ALSO BY SCOTT F. PARKER

As Author

Being on the Oregon Coast
A Way Home: Oregon Essays
Run for Your Life: A Manifesto
The Joy of Running qua Running
Running after Prefontaine: A Memoir

As Editor

Conversations with Ken Kesey
Conversations with Joan Didion
Eminem: Essays on Rap, Poetry, Race
Coffee: Grounds for Debate (with Mike W. Austin)

How to Live

How to Live

A Work in Progress

Scott F. Parker

MMXXI

Some of these aphorisms have appeared previously, sometimes in different forms, in *All Aphorisms, All the Time*;
Whole Beast Rag; *Four and Twenty*; *FragLit*; *What Philosophy Can Tell You about Your Lover* (Open Court, 2012); *in
here* (Monkey Puzzle Press, 2013); and *How to Live: An
Introduction* (Red Bird Chapbooks, 2016).

ISBN: 978-0-9839562-4-2

How to Live

How to Live

Prelude

A familiar story not always comforting. The human being, trembling beneath the burden of being, calls out: *Please.* There is a response. Or perhaps an echo. Or maybe there was no response. The human being is uncertain. The human being—what?—continues . . . and eventually encounters other human beings. They interrupt the silence with words. They speak. One of the humans says to the others, *Let me tell you a story.* They listen. After the story is told, another human says, *Thank you for this story. Here is another.* They go on this way, they go on. And in going on they remain—what?—human . . .

Start where the circle starts.

§ § §

It begins and we are all wonderers.

§ § §

Life itself normative, we justify in circles. The straight line from birth to death an expanding spiral of revisions.

§ § §

Consider the ouroboros. The snake has not eaten its own tail. Nor will it eat its own tail. Rather, the snake *eats* its own tail. Here is what you need to know about the nature of being and becoming, said the artist.

§ § §

The danger of getting one step closer is that eventually we may arrive.

The view from right here. Philosophy never gets off the ground because it's always coming back around to chew on its own feet. That's fine for philosophy. And if the shoe fits, wear it. But we evolved with our feet bare, running and jumping all the while.

§ § §

Thinking about thinking. Even as we dance between tautology and absurdity, still we dance.

§ § §

One history of philosophy: division, division, division—somehow the numerator still undivided.

§ § §

Another history of philosophy: a garden, a café, a walk in the woods—and you need philosophy?

That a philosophy may be true, it must have knowledge of our nature. Our nature: as philosophers in search of knowledge of truth.

§ § §

Philosophy as one of the things we do, as one of the things we are, as one more thing *we* cannot account for.

§ § §

The breakthrough: philosophy is not interested in truth or even in wisdom but in human beings. The breakthrough: *whose?*

§ § §

Game over. The point of a game is to play, but there can only be playing when there is also not playing.

Philosopher's vanity.—The philosopher thinks he sings a verse only because he has not yet made it to the chorus.

§ § §

The philosopher is not merely a kind of artist; he is a kind of artist, but there is no *merely*.

§ § §

First principles: how do we decide to decide to decide to decide which logos is the original logos?

§ § §

Logic at its limits: the difference between something and nothing is something.

§ § §

Maybe the difference between doing and not doing is doing. Or maybe it's not.

It might be necessary from time to time to tear down what has come before and from the remnants build what will come after. There are earthworms among us, those who chew through our waste and make our soil rich, from which the rest of us may blossom. *Hypothetically.*

§ § §

Even what is the case is not necessarily the case— what is or is not the case is the case we make.

§ § §

The power of the seer: to turn cubes into squares, squares into lines, and thoughts into gods.

§ § §

Men make campfires so they may piss on them.

§ § §

Make of this what you will. But do consider the merits of making something.

It is we who are responsible for the world we're born into. *Life, existence, thought,* also *death—being* and *nonbeing*—the *meta* comes first in *metaphysics.*

§ § §

To call a thing "one" is to privilege an arbitrary perspective. To call it "not-one" is to stand elsewhere. To speak is to constrain. To be silent is to never have existed.

§ § §

Three chairs sit unoccupied in Plato's Academy. None of them are real. Fortunately for their sake, they are ignorant of this eternal verity. Later, three philosophers sit upon the chairs. If a chair leg breaks, which philosopher first hits the floor? When I hit the floor, what word is the pain in my ass?

§ § §

Of course. Language is a part of the world not apart from the world.

And yet. The temptation is to think that beyond language lies the real. Terms undefined, referents floating, logic irrelevant, language *problematic*—the real koan is that we locate our concerns in language. The *real* temptation, always already indulged. The real temptation: thought itself.

§ § §

Is this just a story, though, a story a fiction, a fiction a moral? Does telling the right story at the right time in the right way mean knowing what it means?

§ § §

The world is not facts or things; it's facts *and* things. And more. It's more. It's so much more—the definition of art and the cause of the need for it. Art: an answer to itself; a world expanding; the tangled hierarchy of consciousness (or what it means to be human).

Another use-theory of language: there's plenty
outside the text—we just can't talk about it . . . and
that shouldn't bother anyone who isn't looking for
bother. Where we don't have problems, let's allow a
little peace. It's a lovely afternoon.

§ § §

Everything you need to know about how to live you
can learn watching a muskrat chew cattail.

§ § §

That starting line, that diagnostic provocation,
that divisive claim, that fire starter: too often we're
satisfied to explain the world without proceeding to
what the explanation is for, what all culture is for—
figuring out how to be *in the world*.

Already we must say something positive. We must always be prepared to say something positive. In this, we cannot help ourselves. Our epistemologies are constructive, ungrounded but already gaining ground. Thrown into the world. Entropy of no concern within a system. A recursive loop wobbling off its axis. In a void?

§ § §

Whether the relationship between times p and q is fixed and temporally stable or whether there is a time dilation within the system, whether a thing lives in itself or in its relation to something else, ultimately it—ultimately, *everything*—is subsumed by the needs of the author, who himself stands no stiller than a gyroscope. But wait, you say. Does that beg the question? Has the question been begged? The author hears you. He does. But how does he answer you? How?

If we are choosing heroes, what good is a hero who stands still and thinks therefore that the world does too? We must be free to check our watches in real time.

§ § §

A note on chronology: the past actually comes after the present. Forever changing, we never produce it for the same reason twice.

§ § §

Gaining the future. The change we identify is called history. Narrative is always told in retrospect—and yet, *and yet:* time continues to run out.

§ § §

A note on truth: No, I have no note on truth. What kind of note were you expecting? More than once, though, I've done a thing I know I won't regret.

On epistemology. Refusal to sit still. Refusal to go to bed not thinking about tomorrow. Refusal period.

§ § §

A child picks up a stick and draws a line in the sand. A wave washes it away. The child, walking along the beach, picks up another stick and draws a new line. A wave washes it away. With his heel now, the child describes a circle of near-perfect form. A wave washes it away. They go on like this, drawing and washing away, drawing and washing away. An onlooker marvels. Eventually, the onlooker, too, is washed away.

§ § §

On calibration. Caffeinated to the brink of mania, I find my most powerful truths and explode them; any less than that and it's too easy to believe what I tell myself.

We live in the kind of world we find ourselves in. This is not tautology. *Find* doesn't come before *kind* only in the dictionary.

§ § §

Philosophy, like any form of art, wants to make the strange familiar and the familiar strange.

§ § §

To act is to know. There is no coming to terms, finally, with the absurdity of existence—the closest one gets to understanding is full participation, which is the dropping away of terms and the urge for them and of all urges themselves.

§ § §

Favorite words: *wonder, mystery, awe, humility, silence, laughter.* Peace.

On truth and fortune: to hear what one needs to hear when one needs to hear it.

§ § §

Do you suppose, at bottom, human action is the kind of thing that can be understood? Do you suppose we are the ones capable of understanding?

§ § §

How to go meta: X asked Y what he'd learned after all these years. Y said he'd learned that the best answers are those that tend toward edification.

§ § §

Sometimes I think to be fully human is to be willing to live in perpetual confusion. Sometimes I don't think about it at all.

§ § §

Metaphysics in brief. The fundamental component of all existence is momentum.

Contingency (emphasis in original).

§ § §

Life's every moment trails its own history.

§ § §

The being is in the doing. But it's in the undoing as well.

§ § §

Being and nonbeing
Are, one, one
And, two, perspective.

§ § §

Time flows like a river, extends like a dimension, exists in the mind, but is neither river, dimension, nor mental construct—it is the present you don't think twice about accepting.

Directions for opiate use: Infinite supply —> eternal bliss. Just don't overdose.

§ § §

Too much religion is just bad literary criticism.

§ § §

God, the humorist who intended but one consequence: the indelible law of unintended consequences.

§ § §

But just as psychological holes cannot be filled by material goods, so too do psychological needs fail to produce ontic answers.

§ § §

Dreams of gods—epiphenomena of neuron clusters—turtles all the way down. The most effective way to become an atheist is to first become a god.

Nemo ante obitum beatus est. God is happy now or nothing is.

§ § §

I am my own god [feat. Kanye West].

§ § §

Christ, the only Christian; Nietzsche, the only Nietzschean; Kanye, the only one.

§ § §

He who writes for the future doesn't live long enough to discover that the future never arrives. One of the tragedies of human history is that we're not around to witness our deaths.

§ § §

A study of nature. We philosophize out of necessity so that we might live. We live out of necessity so that we might die.

The problem of finitude is not that we know we will die but that for now we are alive.

§ § §

Life's problems are not problems until we make them (problems).

§ § §

You don't have to know Latin to know *Memento mori.*

§ § §

The human being: the fruits of the search for meaning: the search itself.

§ § §

The human meaning: the fruits of the search for being: the search itself.

Look at your wise, your scholars, your artists.
Masters of their domains, they too have to live. And
make all the little compromises survival requires.
Or they don't.

§ § §

One strives in vain to live all of life in a single
go. Living depends on each unique moment being
greeted by its own wisdom.

§ § §

One goal for life: to be there till the end of it.

§ § §

We survive to no avail.

§ § §

All one can do before nothingness is behold it and
engage the tenuousness of existence.

Look closer: there is no model. Write your own manual. We are our own readers.

§ § §

The unabridged story of our species. *Consciousness:* consciousness.

§ § §

Sitting zazen, where is the conclusion of this thought?

§ § §

Who ever learned to hit a ball before taking a swing?

§ § §

When people speak of "people" they speak of themselves.

Go out into the woods, but do not spend your time there—life is not commerce

§ § §

What would a truly natural philosophy look like?

Distinct from what, an unnatural philosophy? What occurs outside nature? Is every sentence a tautology?

§ § §

Know mind, know body, no problem.

§ § §

The human being: a thing beyond itself.

§ § §

I, the only lonely pronoun.

22

Story of self: when grammar becomes metaphysics.

§ § §

To live on the edge is not to live perched above a literal chasm or a metaphorical risk but to track one thought or one breath to its origin and not care whether you fall forever.

§ § §

The *Bildungsroman*, the intermittent trembling before *being*—we've all been there, we all live there.

§ § §

Alone one quiet night coming down off psilocybin, flirting with infinity, everything vanishes. Nothing remains. Then nothing vanishes too.

§ § §

What is the self but a habit, a perspective you've gotten yourself stuck in?

It isn't so much that the self doesn't exist as that it wriggles away from definition. A product of language, but a product nonetheless. It is a story, not a word, and stories exist in a state of constant change until they end.

§ § §

And yet, what is the project of life if not to cultivate—through acts, through decisions, through reactions to contingency—the self?

§ § §

A self can be a good thing to have. No, the tongue doesn't taste itself. But it can taste everything else. And that's not all it can do.

Reflections in a broken mirror. How can I assemble the self when I don't even recognize the pieces, when I'm not sure if they're from one set or a multitude, when I can't determine whether there's a cohesive picture waiting or just an infinity of angles, perspectives, fragments of fragments?

§ § §

I'm suddenly flashing back to a confused night when I tapped on a window for twenty minutes trying to get your attention before I realized I was standing in front of a mirror.

§ § §

The self is a mirror disguised as a window. Trying to look through it we're always looking in. And reflecting back out and in. A series, a regress, a trap. Spring.

§ § §

The objects of our attention become the subject of our attending.

Another true story brought to you by mushrooms: I saw and did not recognize myself in the mirror. Q: What does "true" mean in this context?

§ § §

All breathing is autobiography.

§ § §

Take as many showers as you like, you will never wash the blood of your birth from your skin.

§ § §

Aging means letting go of infinite possibility. So does birth.

§ § §

There is no perfection but the perfection of imperfection.

And even if there is no perfection, I want it anyway.

§ § §

It is not always wasteful to state the obvious: we are addicted to our suffering.

§ § §

Adulthood: the day you realize there's no such thing.

§ § §

How to live peacefully and even forever: remember: you are going to die. You can't remind yourself of this too much. Or be concerned by it too little.

§ § §

Corpse pose: my yoga is the shoe slowly wearing its tread to smooth rubber nothing; my yoga is the work remaining to be done; my yoga is the answer to the question of what we pass along from one generation to the next.

The only true and constant presence in life: death—
an absence.

§ § §

What haven't we outsourced when we take our
phones from our pockets to find out if we're still
alive?

§ § §

You will die your own death. Your iPhone will not
save you.

§ § §

Life is: *easy come, easy go?*

§ § §

Minding death (your own), is your life a book you
want to read, a party you want to attend?

Montaigne, Cicero—they were right: to philosophize
is to learn how to die. But they would have been just
as right to say that to live is to learn how to die. To
live any other way is to already be dead.

§ § §

Making of today the means toward tomorrow's end
will help you sleep when you want to sleep—but
what helps you when you need to stay awake?

§ § §

I pursue silence. Thoughts link with thoughts
to form a chain leading into the void, enfolding.
The trick is to get to where you can't tell if you're
inventing the future or unfolding it. I lie suspended,
a bridge between existence and non-.

We have no recourse to truth, only to utility, and Nietzsche says, "No small art is it to sleep: it is necessary for that purpose to keep awake all day." If this is an art, I want to craft paradox—and breathe presence in absence, maintain awareness of the exact moment when form and emptiness dissolve.

§ § §

Call thinking binary or dissolution ultimately synthetic, an emptiness beyond the emptiness that makes form possible, I still want to sleep with eyes open and witness my own annihilation. The period when you can't tell if you're awake or asleep is the best time to ask yourself: Why is there something rather than nothing? And what is the ontological nature of time? The circle circles itself. And a question asked in words cannot be answered in anything else.

§ § §

These logics are nontransferable.

Skillful in the means of contra-diction within the
fiction of my chosen -ism.

§ § §

These memories occur in language. This language
occurs in context. This context is given. This given
is got.

§ § §

Tear the system down and only the system remains.

§ § §

Further notes on contingency. What results when
the history of histories your existence is the summit
of comes crumbling down, whether in a singular
insight punch or in the slow and steady erosion
of mountainous assumptions? Where are you left
standing? Whatever else your foundation is it is
preparing itself to give way.

We do not become who we are. We are who we are and we become who we become.

§ § §

Wisdom of logic./Logic of wisdom. The good is that at which action, by definition, aims. All human beings seek, by assumption, happiness. Happiness is, by syllogism, *the* good. That means the mean of our means don't mean we are mean, as in cruel—but dear god how we fail to flourish.

§ § §

ipso facto foolio—Evidence of choice, evidence of a chain-linked fence, tautology in a shopping bag. Who chooses the chooser who chooses the chooser who chooses the chooser?

§ § §

Who is the narrator's narrator? Who directs the experience?

If you've chosen, how did you choose? And how did you choose how to choose? And how did you choose how to choose how to choose? & + 1 etc. —And we are all finite moments on an infinite chain. Regress this way with me.

§ § §

Sanity—when the insanities you locate in yourself correspond to those others locate in you.

§ § §

We tell ourselves li(v)es in order to live.

§ § §

On what is and what is not a paradox: every story sounding in your head is a lie, including this one.

§ § §

There's always more to be said on reification, but none of it ever survives editing.

Imagine the experience of your own non-existence, the existence of your own non-experience. And then, may we suggest a walk?

§ § §

To be unknown but also be known as unknown—at least to oneself.

§ § §

Neti neti or the impossibility of self-examination. The logical implication is *nonduality*, but I can hardly bring myself to type something so crass, so *self*-defeating.

§ § §

On emptiness. To become fully who you are when you do not exist is to dance where the beat beats.

Know thyself well enough to know when to stop trying to know thyself. There is a black hole in each of us. The trick is recognize this without getting sucked in.

§ § §

What is the self? A tidy question does not presume a tidy answer, or any. The most dangerous traps are the ones we set for ourselves. The best response is often a change of subject, if you will.

§ § §

It is not enough for there to be not-I—for there to be I there must be you.

§ § §

If there were no other, I would be forced to invent you.

When we say "I" to each other we say two distinct things. It's not that one concept applies to two specific cases. There are as many concepts as there are cases.

§ § §

We needn't feel alone to choose to be together.

§ § §

Every letter is a love letter.

§ § §

Sometimes accepting a gift is the most generous thing you can do.

§ § §

Let friends never speak of loyalty.

Just as circumstances never repeat in this life, so too must one's actions and ideas overcome the past.

§ § §

It's too easy to take credit for the moral achievements of others.

§ § §

A moral voice is necessarily an unpopular one.

§ § §

Meaning like morality is situational.

§ § §

I was lucky. I had an uncle who taught me that the economy is merely a component of ecology.

Between the utilitarian and the deontologist lies
the fact that when tomorrow comes you will stand
in front of a mirror and decide when it is time to
blink.

§ § §

If god is dead, and if your father is dead, and even if
you yourself are already dead: Is your son yet dead?
Is your son yet born? If ethics means anything, it
means this.

§ § §

Our individual contingencies are necessarily
particular, but the *necessity of* our contingencies is
universal.

§ § §

Moral judgments are always normative. A claim
is being made about how to live, backed by the
promise of more living, then dying, and after dying
only death.

Buddhism as a way of thinking. Taoism as a way of living. The grace to know when to think and when to live.

§ § §

When you find yourself sitting for the first time at the foot of an oak tree reading about the *a priori* and the *a posteriori* you'll think to yourself that you've made it somewhere. And you have. The question is how much your butt hurts and whether the acorn will land on your head.

§ § §

I don't read books to understand them; I read them to cannibalize them—I take only what I need and leave the rest for scavengers.

§ § §

Coffee drips like blood from my teeth as I eat the world alive from the desk in my study.

Gifts. Reading the right book at the right time has given me so many opportunities *to hope*.

§ § §

Your butt, your back, your shoulders become sore only when the book in front of you is out of alignment.

§ § §

Sound advice is distinguished less by the quality of the advice than by the quality of the sound.

§ § §

Not all texts are self-aware. Imagine an author drawn to the sound of conclusion but whose ear is greedy and whose memory is short. Imagine him unable to conclude his conclusions until his yearning eventually becomes the sound of his listening.

What this book is going to be about. It's going to be about how to live. A set of maxims. Very practical. It's just now coming to the point. It's nearly there.

§ § §

So many sentences that will never be finished, so many ideas unrecorded, so much written on lost scraps of paper, so much material without form.

§ § §

Why aphorisms? Because the thoughts come when they come only as they come. Why aphorisms? We hasten to return to the silence that envelops these words. Why aphorisms? Everything they don't say.

§ § §

This aphorism has been left from the page— courageously, mind you.

Close-enough syllogism. The memoirist's purpose: to write the self into being. All writing is autobiography. ∴ *Voila!*

§ § §

If sanity means having a story of self that is compatible with "reality," in a changing world the only universal story is the story of selflessness—the ur-self, the un-self—and telling this story to oneself is the way.

§ § §

The essayist—the good one—tries on ideas, looking for one that fits, knowing all along that none finally will.

§ § §

Literature: writing that means more than it says.

A note on process. In retrospect we know how to write when we begin. What we learn from doing it is what the writing was for.

§ § §

To write is to hold oneself to the awful flame of self-consumption, burning the stuff of I into the product of me—that *I* must be sturdy lest it melt and become deformed; and the only stable thing is that which cannot be broken—that which doesn't exist in the first place. An artist must find and write from that place which because it didn't hold anything can never be emptied.

§ § §

A writer's day is never over—every moment is one with the words on the page.

§ § §

Fantasy/nightmare? When self-consumption consumes itself.

That nonbeing would preclude suffering—yes. That death would relieve it—yes. That we have a right to suicide—of course. That we should consider it—absolutely. That we should go through with it—I want to say *no*. I want to say that only by reflecting regularly on death do we find reasons to live.

§ § §

You will die. In a hundred years everyone you know will be dead. Your children's bodies will rot. Your grandchildren will be eaten by worms. Go now and make something. Beauty is possible in this world or not at all.

§ § §

Implicit in beauty, its sine qua non: In any case, you will soon be dead.

Every text a manifesto written in blood. How many writers have said writing is the mania by which I don't kill myself? How many forgot to?

§ § §

A state of controlled mania wherein the world begins to feed itself of itself prior to shooting exponentially into the absolute zero of annihilation, and you are the valve, the only valve.

§ § §

Fingers rest on keys as the cat waits for a squeak to become a mouse.

§ § §

A message from Montaigne's cat: the writer must do the impossible on every page: become the other.

§ § §

Writing: preparation for death?

45

When Cynthia Gooding said to Bob Dylan that "Death of Emmett Till" "doesn't have any sense of being written. It sounds as if it just came out."

§ § §

It is crucial to master one's craft, but to stop there is forever to play by someone else's rules.

§ § §

A brief commentary on originality:

> Even in Kyoto—
> hearing the cuckoo's cry—
> I long for Kyoto.
>   —Basho

> Even in Portland—
> gray clouds obscuring mountain—
> I long for Portland.
>   —After Basho

No individual making considered decisions in the
blank background of life, the world given for the
subject, and the voices we speak into the void not
ours alone but all of ours—we carry everything with
us—and maybe we will build something of our own
but the material is borrowed.

§ § §

We are like feathers on a bird to poets, she
supposes.

§ § §

Lesson learned . . . and learned . . . and learned
. . . and learned: our failures of empathy are
fundamentally failures of imagination.

§ § §

Empathy is always a risk without which art is not.

Tony Hoagland wonders if the artistic life begins in play and ends in ambition. But death comes when it comes.

§ § §

Artistic outlook. There is meaning. And if there isn't, there will be!

§ § §

Art a gift that doesn't stop giving—life as a kind of art.

§ § §

To be superficial: to feel apprehension before one's love of beautiful skin.

§ § §

Aesthetics is about how you look your lover in the eye and when you are able to open yourself to consequences you cannot foresee. Your life in freefall, the present moment alone holding you up. Do not *study* beauty.

The generation that was so efficient it used up all its time.

§ § §

Enjoy the sunset. Your grandchildren's grandchildren will soon be dead.

§ § §

Love is the most selfish emotion says the one man in the room who has never given love.

§ § §

By necessity. When love is increasingly needed it is also increasingly hard to come by.

§ § §

If you are lucky enough to discover what you need more than anything, it's this that it is your responsibility to give.

Love is like trigonometry. For some, it comes easily. For others, life is a cram session for an infinite series of pop quizzes.

§ § §

And don't the benefits of love occur independently of love's object?

§ § §

The sources of ourselves are forever mysterious. But whatever the causes of our condition, the experience of it remains, and so the question becomes: given our circumstances, how should we be?

§ § §

The mere impression of effortlessness.

§ § §

To be someone who works hard and accomplishes much without ever straining.

To make things look so easy that in time they become so.

§ § §

To be someone who accepts his fortunes as well as his failures.

§ § §

To be ignited and then to ignite.

§ § §

To not make simple things complicated and to not make complicated things (too) simple.

§ § §

Two roads diverged in a wood, and so the story continued.

What are the ends of a life? It's end. A tentative
definition of happiness: when the means are
the ends, meaning the end, meaning the circle
expanding for the time being.

§ § §

Some people look for answers. And don't some
prefer questions?

§ § §

In the beginning was the void. In the void was
being. And in being was the beginning.

§ § §

Being, again: a haunt, ours *to wander.*

§ § §

Begin again. With luck we remain as we were:
wonderers.

And end where the circle ends.

Scott F. Parker wishes you well.